# THE
# ENABLED BODY
## A CALL TO UNITY IN THE BODY OF CHRIST

Copyright ©2021 Angie Elaine V. Coote.
All rights reserved.
Published in the United Kingdom. A catalogue record for this book is available from the British Library.
ISBN 978-1-913455-37-8
No part of this book shall be reproduced or transmitted in any form or by any means, electronic or mechanical, including photocopying, recording, or by any information retrieval system without prior written permission of the publisher.
Published by Scribblecity Publications.
Printed in Great Britain.
Although every precaution has been taken in the preparation of this book, the publisher and author assume no responsibility for errors or omissions. Neither is any liability assumed for damages resulting from the use of this information contained herein.

DEDICATION

To Dr. Chukwudi Onyali
Pastor of *The Abiding Word Ministries*
&
Pastor Elizabeth (Pastor Liz) Ozo-Onyali
*Founder of The Women of Purpose Ministries*

# PREFACE

It was June of 2019 when I walked into my *kairos* moment. I was called out by Apostle Dr. Chukwudi Ozo-Onyali of The Abiding Word Ministries (T.A.W.M.), who laid hands on me, and by divine impartation, I experienced my spirit renewed and recharged with a fresh fire.

This book was birthed out of that impartation which awakened my spirit and all that had been dormant for years.

God is supernatural, and the way he orchestrates his plans, are unfathomable. He is forgiving, loving, compassionate, faithful, full of mercy and grace. He has equipped his kingdom citizens with gifts to operate within the local assemblies. This is clearly stated in Paul's exhortation in *Ephesians 4:7-16*.

> *"But unto every one of us is given grace according to the measure of the gift of Christ. Wherefore he saith, when he ascended up on high, he led captivity captive, and gave gifts unto men...And he gave some, apostles; and some, prophets; and some evangelists; and some, pastors and teachers; For the perfecting of the saints, for the work of the ministry, for the edifying of the body of Christ: Till we all come in the unity of the faith, and of the knowledge of the Son of God, unto a perfect man, unto the measure of the stature of the fullness of Christ; That we henceforth be no more children, tossed to and fro, carried about with every wind of doctrine, by the sleight of men, and cunning craftiness, whereby they lie in wait to deceive; But speaking the truth in love, may grow up into him in all things, which is the head, even*

*Christ: From whom the whole body fitly joined together and compacted by that which every joint supplieth, according to the effectual working in the measure of every part, maketh increase of the body unto the edifying of itself in love.*

## A Guide to the spiritual Anatomy of the body of Christ -Teaching Exposé

This Bible exposé came about from what I learnt in Anatomy and Physiology class. The illustration of the body parts, structures and functions intrigued me especially when we were assigned in different groups and given a body part to research. I got the cheek bone (Zygomatic or beauty bone) and we did a presentation.

Enjoy the lyrics and rhythm of our cheek bone:

> *My bone my bone, my beauty bone...*
> *Dancing to the rhythm of my beauty bone,*
> *Known as the Zygomatic bone My bone, my bone my cheek bone,*
> *Dancing to the rhythm of my zygomatic beauty bone.*
> *Vamos Amigo my Zygomatic bone,*
> *Vamos Amiga my beauty bone...My bone, my bone...*
> *Adios Amigas, my Zygomatic Bone.*

Ideas came as I read Ezekiel chapter 37:1-14. The bones in the valley are analogies or representations likening the body of Christ, His bride, the Church coming together in unity and completeness.

I was ecstatic with my findings as the Holy Spirit gave me fresh revelations through prayer.

The skeletal structure is a perfect outline of our human make up. The photographic illustration of our extremities, for example: Our arms if detached from the shoulder blades (clavicle and scapula) is useless. A dislocated elbow from the complete arm (humerus and ulnar bones) serves no purpose on its own. What help can the fingers (digits), palm (phalanges, metacarpals, and carpals) do when removed?

We are all called in one enabled body for transformation and completeness with a chain of command, Unity! Paul exhorted on the vision in Corinthians chapter 4:1-27, making emphasis of the physical body.
I believe Paul's desire is that our generation be empowered on the revelation to mature us.

There are reasons why the physical body is used as examples in scriptures, as the emphasis is on how we should be spiritually connected; to serve each other using our vocation, calling for building up and encouraging all body parts. Elohim's kingdom agenda is inclusive of unity for completeness within the body of Christ.

The strongest bone in the body is the femur (thigh) and without the purpose of this bone the knee (patella) could not align with the bone of the leg (Tibia and Fibula). These two bones coordinating for the completion and movements of the foot, muscles included.

The muscles are hidden underneath the skin (epithelial organ), and without the importance of the muscles, movements would be hindered. Walking without the heel (Calcaneus) or the digits of the toes (tarsals, metatarsal, and phalanges) the feet would not function on their own. So, it is with every person within the body of Christ. Our uniqueness varies and are diverse.

Some are hidden like the 'comely parts' that we cannot see because flesh and muscles are protecting the bones and the internal organs of the physical body.

Can we see a capillary? These are tiny thread like veins that are embedded in the muscles, yet if one stream of capillary is ruptured, it causes much damage to the functionality of the body just like a vein that is much bigger.

The anatomy of the body is interestingly comparing to the anatomy of the spiritual body. The inferior needs the superior to work together, and the term "inferior" should not be taken in a negative way. Everyone has an important position or groove that no one else can fit into and function in but you.

Your mold is carved out, so, get ready and excited to learn about you and your specific body part. You were born to grow and develop, maturing both physically, and transforming into the spiritual mature stature becoming the betroth bride of Christ.

It is maturity time, let us go on a journey of physical and spiritual education.

My head, my shoulders, my knees, my toes, God made them all.

Blessings and illumination to our minds as we gain clear focus.

Shalom

Author / Contributor
Angie Elaine V. Coote

# TABLE OF CONTENTS

Preface     v

Introduction     11

*Chapter 1*
    How Do You Function?     19

*Chapter 2*
    Growing in the Vine     24

*Chapter 3*
    For The Body Is Not One Member But Many Parts 1     26

*Chapter 4*
    For The Body Is Not One Member But Many Parts 2     29

*Chapter 5*
    For The Body Is Not One Member But Many part 3     33

*Chapter 6*
    For The Body Is Not One Member But Many part 4     36

*Chapter 7*
    For The Body Is Not One Member But Many part 5     40

*Chapter 8*
    The Power of Unity     43

*Chapter 9*
    Every Body Part is Important     46

*Chapter 10*
    What is Your Purpose?    49

*Chapter 11*
    Knowing the Purpose of the Arms And Hands 1    53

*Chapter 12*
    Knowing the Purpose of the Arms And Hands 2    55

*Chapter 13*
    Care for One another    58

*Chapter 14*
    The Different Ministerial Gifts Part 1    62

*Chapter 15*
    The Different Ministerial Gifts Part 2    66

*Chapter 16*
    The Different Ministerial Gifts Part 3    70

*Chapter 17*
    The Different Ministerial Gifts Part 4    74

*Chapter 18*
    Being Effective in Our Gifts    85

*Chapter 19*
    The Holy Spirit Our Helper    87

*Chapter 20*
    Summary    90

# INTRODUCTION
## The Skeletal Systems (Allegory)
*Memory Verse: John 15:1-17*

Elohim, the Lord of creation walked into Wynter's Career of Nursing (WCO), His hand was upon Psychiatry, Anatomy & Physiology, and the fundamentals of Nursing, guiding the tutors in the classrooms like a valley of framework. The Scholars who had come from wide and far were filled with despair like bones without bodies. Elohim saw these skeletal systems in the classroom, looking dull and lifeless. He asked them, *"Tutors of W.C.O. can these skeletal systems be restored and educated?* They replied, "O sure master, you give us the instructions to impart, nothing is impossible with you."

Then He said to them, *"Speak, teach, educate these skeletal systems, and shine the light in darkness. Tell them, listen, observe, and learn psychiatry, anatomy & physiology that compliments fundamentals of nursing. I will breath in them and cause them to exhale, expand and relax. Inspiration will enter them; they will be motivated.I will attach tendons to their joints. Make epithelial come upon them and cover them with dermis and epidermis. They will inhale and exhale, they will start to move, expand, and learn, then they will know I created anatomy, psychiatry, that compliments fundamentals of nursing. This is the start of the restoration process."*

As the Tutors; Mr Wynter, Mr Thomas and Mrs Reynolds-Rowe took turns teaching according to the schedule, giving out information as Elohim had commanded. Suddenly Knowledge increased, laughter and rejoicing were heard. Visions illuminated; minds renewed. Bones start to connect together, tendons and epithelial & connective tissues, start to receive life. The nervous systems began to coordinate and correspond with the brain. Muscular tissues start their processes under the integumentary system. However, some 'bodies' were still not responding? The creator said, *"it seems, many are experiencing psychomotor retardation. They are moving too slow and they have a long way to go. All five senses need to operate and communicate; the visual, the auditory, the tactile, the olfactory and the gustatory need to cooperate. No more hallucinations and delusions. Alert knowledge, sharpen understanding, go forth wisdom, impart and instruct these skeletal systems."*

The Teachers began to do as they were commanded. Then their extremities came to life and stood up on their **femurs**, (thigh bone) **patella**, (kneecap) **tibias**, (shinbones) **fibulas**, (leg bone on lateral side) **tarsals**, (metatarsals, and phalanges).

Then he said unto them. *"Oh, tutors of WCO, these are the prospective scholars I will send forth into the society and the nations to work while it is day."*

Though they had doubted, cussed and at times their faith grew weak, they lament "Our **serous** (fluid) have dried up, our brains are losing their cells!" Nevertheless, dementia must go! *"I renew brain cells and perform healings everywhere possible. I have opened up your intellects, restored your minds, breathe in your intercostal muscles oxygen, and empowered you all with knowledge. Read your ethics of nursing. Try to prevent sicknesses and practice proper hygiene. Work to help alleviate pain and* *suffering and the preservation of life. I create and structure you to function in many special and complex ways."*

## Skeletal Restoration of the Body of Christ
Ezekiel and the Valley of Bones
Ezekiel 37: 1-14

*"The hand of the LORD was on me, and he brought me out by the Spirit of the LORD and set me in the middle of a valley; it was full of bones. 2 He led me back and forth among them, and I saw a great many bones on the floor of the valley, bones that were very dry. 3 He asked me, "Son of man, can these bones live?"*

The same way is the divine hand of the creator upon his apostles, prophets, evangelist, pastors, teachers. There was a spiritual awakening for the five-fold ministry within the body of Christ, with such the Holy Spirit guided them into all the nations of the earth. As they travelled, they saw valleys of framework, scattered across the globe: East, West, North and South. The People that came from everywhere, looked just like skeletal structures, dislocated, separated, tossed to and fro, dried out because of discouragements, despair, frustration, depression, drained or sucked out and left dying or already dead. Corpse, corpse, there are impossibilities everywhere.

As the heavenly Father led his servants back and forth among these structures, he asked "*My disciples, leaders, servants, you are called, appointed, and anointed. Can these skeletal structures be restored or resurrected (brought back to spiritual life?).*

They replied, "Mighty Jehovah, Creator of the universe, of all living creatures, You can do all things."

Then he responded: "*You were like them once, Now I have raised you up to speak my words, declare, decree, prophecy, educate, shout out to the corners of the nations what I have deposited in you. Release it in the earth! Speak to the East, the west, to the North and the South my sons and daughters. It is time to illuminate, shine through the darkness. Blow my words as a trumpet in Zion, sound my alarm upon my holy hill. Cry out, oh my warriors, use what I have given you. Let them know, be willing and obedient. I will cause them to inhale and exhale. Expand, stretch, strengthen and lengthen the coast of your borders. The newness of my resurrection power will be activated.*

*I will attach tendons to their joints, make fresh epithelial (flesh) tissues grow again and cover them with clean flesh. They will inhale and exhale the fresh breath of my Spirit. They will move about by faith. The knowledge of me will illuminate their minds pulling down every stagnant, negative, inferior imaginations. They will start to believe and recognize me through you my harvesters, that this is their restoration season."*

As these servant workers, disciples obeyed the master's instruction and began doing as they were commanded, they saw different levels of manifestations of the Creator's authority taking form within the body. Miracles were performed. Healings and deliverances were wrought, knowledge increased, praise, worship, joy, laughter, and rejoicing were coming from all over the nations. Visions illuminated, minds renewed as brain cells regenerated, frames were stronger and rejuvenated by the living water of life and the wind of His Spirit.

Bones were connecting, tendons and epithelial (flesh) and connective tissues began to coordinate with the word. Muscular tissues began their process under the anointing and quickening of the Logos and Rhema of God.
However, some members were still looking lame, lifeless.

The Creator said: *"It seems many of my people are still lukewarm, they must be either cold or hot. It is not my desire to refuse or reject anyone. They need to be alert, awaken from their spiritual slumber and arise to the break of a new dawn. They need the fire of my Holy Spirit power. Their senses need to be revived and their vision sharp like the eagle. They need full corporation to be unified. No more frustration, complacency, and passiveness. My Spirit that I send is able to impart knowledge, sharpen their understanding and wisdom.*

*Impart and instruct them my servants. They shall live and not die. They shall declare my mighty works in the land of the living. These are the Joshua generation that I am restoring. The Elijah spirit in these last days. Oh, my Apostles, Prophets, Pastors, Teachers and Evangelist, I have chosen many within the body of Christ. Many have faltered, gone astray, wondered away from the fold. I have come back for the prodigals. The tempter's snare must be broken by my power over and in their lives.*

*I have poured out my Spirit, restoring all your members. Empowered you with my gifts and callings. Now it is* time to manifest my fruit and replenish the dry arears with *my living water. You should no more be scattered. I sent forth unity so you can function in many special and complex ways to bring glory to me.*

This simple Sunday school song sums it all up.

Ezekiel call them dry bones,
Ezekiel call them dry bone, now hear he the word of the Lord.
And the head bone connected to the neck bone,
and the neck bone connected to the backbone,
The backbone connected to thigh bone.
The thigh bone connected to the knee bone,
The knee bone connected to the leg bone,
The leg bone connected to the foot bone,
now hear he the word of the Lord!

The foot bone connected to the leg bone,
The leg bone connected to the knee bone,
The knee bone connected to thigh bone,
The thigh bone connected to the backbone,
The backbone connected to the head bone,
Oh, hear the word of the Lord!

Chapter 1

# HOW DO YOU FUNCTION?

## Skeletal Restoration of the Body of Christ
*Memory Verse: Galatians 5:24*

Do we know our own body parts and their functions? If we do not know what we are moving around in and with, we are incapacitating our own purpose of living. We are sabotaging our own selves for lack of knowledge to the importance of living and who are we living for in this body and the reason we are saved through the blood of Jesus Christ, -Yeshua Hamashiach's identity.
Galatians 5:24: *"And they that are Christ's have crucified the flesh and the affections and lusts."*

A lot depends on us, there is work and a choice. Jesus did the finished work on the cross leading us into salvation (deliverance) but it's based on conditions, we have to do our part. This trains us to take responsibility and be accountable.

We are called to be stewards and ambassadors. We are his representatives in the earth realm as we live out His Kingdom mandate authority.

Verse 25: *"If we live in the Spirit, let us also walk in the Spirit."* *
This verse challenges us that it is possible, and the solution is here in the blueprint of his word. We are saved to be spiritual beings though we are living in a fleshly body, and the amount of time we spend in his word determines how we accomplish such. The Holy Spirit is given to help us if we allow him.

Verse 26; *"avoiding the desires of vain glory, provoking one another, envying one another."* We have a responsibility to care and watch over each other as we all belong to one body. Do we not care for our natural bodies once we have grown and matured?

When we were babies, we had adults who took care of us, supervised us as our brain was still developing. Time and time again we would do foolish things, stumble and fall over, the natural determination to walk is in our DNA, no matter the cuts and bruises, we would stubbornly rise up and go back to our game. We would continuously stagger, trying to hold on, as we reach out to grip the nearest object or person. That was part of the stages of life.

Welcome to our Christian maturity! In our walk, when feeding, we had to start somewhere on the nipple bottle first, drinking up the milk of the word until our stomachs can manage solid food. Can we see the way our natural growth transitions like the spiritual growth? As we mature, we bathe, dress and daily choose what we eat.

Just as we have the natural laws and the spiritual laws. The Physical-temporal goes hand in hand with our spiritual growth. We can draw parallels as we will examine the 9 Types of Body Systems:

1. The Muscle skeletal System- Support and protect the body.
2. The Digestive (Gastrointestinal /food bag, gut) process the foods and eliminates waste (undigested process nutrients)
3. The Respiratory- absorbs in oxygen in the body and rids the body of carbon dioxide.
4. The Circulatory/Cardiovascular or Transportation (The Heart) takes the nutrients, oxygen that is absorbed in the blood stream all over the entire body and transport hormones(chemicals) secreted by ductless glands.
5. The Endocrine: produces hormones (chemical secretes

by ductless glands which provides communication between the organs of the body.

6. The Nervous system: provides communication and control the functions of the body.

7. The Urinary System: Controls the fluid balance and the electrolytes, as well as rid the body of waste (in the form of urine).

8. Integumentary (the skin) provides a protective covering, also stores fat, and nutrients and also rids the body of waste during perspiration. The skin also regulate the body's temperature.

9. Reproductive – Produces together the human body and develops sexual identity.

*Note:* The stomach contains nine organs: Basic cavity; the mouth, Pharynx(throat), Esophagus(gullet), stomach (gut), small intestines, large intestines, (colon) Liver, Gall bladder, Pancreas. The body of Christ is a spiritual kingdom. Living in the earthly flesh or carnal realm alone will not allow us to understand the spiritual substance of how divinely we fit. The enemy of our soul opposes us daily. He left his first estate, so he will try all he can to keep us from our spiritual inheritance.

Let us be determined with the help of the Holy Spirit to

be transformed by the renewing of our minds, Romans 12:2. Imagine it to be like having new brains cells grow in the name of Jesus. We need his mind in us daily, just as 1 Cor 2:16 states that we have the mind of Christ. Come on, we can do it! His grace is sufficient in our weaknesses.

He gives beauty for ashes, strength for fear, gladness for sorrow and hope in despair. Get up! Get up! Get up! It is a new dawn! A Fresh wind is blowing our way! Fresh Fire! Illumination cometh from Elohim's breath, Inhale His freshness now and exhale his healing power so others can live!

## Reflections:

Our natural gifts, talents and skills are a type of shadow to the kingdom gifts. We were born with natural abilities that need to develop, and many need training to develop such abilities to be able to function both in the secular and spiritual kingdom.

With the help of the Holy Spirit, transformation into spirituality, is enhanced and sharpened during one's conversion. just as we belong to His body we are also branches in the vine.

Chapter 2

# GROWING IN THE VINE

Skeletal Restoration of the Body of Christ
*Memory Verse: John 15:1-17*

Who is the Vine? Who are the branches? The Vine and the branches are a symbol of growth, bearing fruits that remain. You need to be planted in the vine, Christ, in order to regenerate and be fruitful. John 15:4 *"No branch can bear fruit by itself; it must remain in the vine. Neither can you bear fruit unless you remain in me."* God's desire is that we bear both physical and spiritual fruit, and as we remain in him, the word assures us we will be fruitful, v:5 *"If you remain in me and I in you, you will bear much fruit."*

Importantly, the universe exists because of a Divine being in active presence. An all-powerful One that put all things together. In him we live and move and have our being (Acts 17:28)

Even though we are all one body grafted in the vine, the uniqueness of each human fingerprint assures us that we are all individually crafted to fit in our own cavity. We are to be comfortable in our own skin, personality, as we become more like our Savior Jesus Christ.

Welcome to the era of regrowing new wings to soar like the eagle! 1 Corinthians 2:9, But as it is written: No eye has seen, no ear has heard, and no mind has imagined what God has prepared for those who love him.

## Reflections:

God desires that our spiritual body is also complete with the gifts and callings, to enable us to function effectively in our spheres of influence.

Are you missing a natural body part? There are different body part replacements that have been manufactured in the natural. Just imagine, if God the Creator gave mankind great ideas to be creative in the natural, think about the creative miracles he has in store in his heavenly manufacturing company!
Capture the BIG picture. He desire us to be his heirs to benefit in all his kingdom requirements. Do we not all

Chapter 3

# FOR THE BODY IS NOT ONE MEMBER BUT MANY PARTS 1
*Memory Verse: I Corinthians 12:14*

Think about the complexities and diversities of our natural body parts. Researchers and Scientist have documented that approximately two hundred and six (206) bones make up the complete body. If we were to itemize each bone structure in our body, we will learn the names of each. That is so exciting! If our bones could talk verbally, we would be scared, right?

The way we treat our body, at times taking it for granted, yet we use and need it daily to move around, stretch, bend, reach for things, eat, sleep, and all other daily activities. Do we really observe all parts of our bodies? Do we pause and take each part into consideration? Do we care for one particular part less than the rest? So often we do, mentally, psychologically, yes! Think of how we abuse our health? Overeating and ingesting poor nutrition without concern for the nutritional value of each food item we consume on a daily basis. We even forget to do basic exercises to keep the bones lubricated and flexible. Until some repercussion arises.

A few weeks ago, I got up early, spent some time communing with my heavenly Father, then sat and typed for hours. I felt soreness in my left arm from the shoulder, biceps, triceps to my elbow. I ignored the slight discomfort for a while and went to the bathroom, and realized my arm was like lead! I cried out in aching pain. I lifted my left arm with the right one as the pain was excruciating. It took me fifteen minutes to pull my pajama top off using the same method I used to assist the elderly. I went inside the shower and my arm was not able to wash under my right axilla/armpit. I moaned and groaned crying out to Abba father. I wondered how many people were experiencing similar aches and pains.

What wicked cruelty, to feel such awful discomfort with a body part! Through prayers and confessing the word the Lord revealed to me the consequence of my action to my one arm. All the pressure on one part of the body can be so detrimental.

**Reflections:**

If one body part suffers, the other feels it. We are all a part of God's body, we need each other to survive. We should never harm each other with words from our mouth.

Let us be reminded that we are called into one body, and allow others to develop and share the physical load or ministerial work.

All body parts are essential to each other. No one individual body part was called to do everything.

Chapter 4

# FOR THE BODY IS NOT ONE MEMBER BUT MANY PARTS 2
*Memory Verse: I Corinthians 12:14*

*"If the foot shall say, because I am not the hand, I am not of the body; is it therefore not of the body?"*
What if the foot is where the hand had been, and the hand where the foot should be? Not only would it make a hilarious sight, it would be so confusing and create a severe malfunctioning of the body.

Do we wake and decide we do not need one of our body parts? Oh, feet, today I will do without you until some other time. Getting down on the floor, you are "trying to manage" with just your hands. What strain, pressure, challenge and most off all stress you would encounter.

Elohim the Creator knew what he was doing in designing each body part. He placed them strategically where each belongs and serves its unique purpose. Think of certain persons born with disabilities? Some without a limb or limbs, and the ability to be mobile. Some are given adaptive aides or artificial limb to aid the support, the artificial replacement is attached exactly where that body part is missing. The foot is important to the whole body. Treat your feet to pedicure. Pamper your feet naturally. Take care of the nail fungus or buildup of callous, bunions or corns. The feet are important to the body.

Let us thank God for the importance of the feet of those who go places many of us are not called to go. Pray, and give support.
Psalm 18: 29,33, 36 & 38,
Verse 29: *"For by thee I have run through a troop and by thee I have leaped over a wall."*
Verse 33: *"He maketh my feet like hinds' feet, and setteth me upon my high places."*
Verse 36: *"Thou hast enlarged my steps under me, that my feet did not slip."*
Verse 38: *"I have wounded them that they were not able to rise: they are fallen under my feet."*

**Relections:**
Our feet is not for running mischief, Proverbs 6:16. We need our feet strong, healthy to move with the gospel of peace. Isaiah 52:7, *"How lovely on the mountains are the feet of Him who brings good news, announcing peace, proclaiming good news of happiness, our God reigns."*

**Prayer:**
I love my feet, and I praise God my creator for strength to run this race with patience. I will not use my feet for evil, kick or stomp on anyone but the devil.

I will rest my feet and elevate whenever necessary for moderate circulation. I will give my feet proper skin care, take care of the nails and cuticle. I will wear the proper fitted shoe or sandal. I thank you heavenly Father I will not walk any contaminated grounds or walk to go do evil. My heels will not be ensnared by any satanic shackles or nets. By the blood of Jesus Christ, all satanic landmines are defused from any grounds and property or wherever I walk in Jesus Name.

Psalm 91:13
*"Though shalt tread upon the adder: the young lion and the dragon shalt thou trample under feet."*

My feet shall not lead me into mischief in Jesus mighty name. My feet are penetrated with the fire of the living God! His potent superior blood encircles my feet and surrounding. His angels encamp round about me.

Chapter 5

# FOR THE BODY IS NOT ONE MEMBER BUT MANY PARTS 3

*Memory Verse: I Corinthians 12:16*

*"And if the ear shall say, because I am not the eye, I am not of the body. Is it therefore not of the body?"*

The ear is made of different sections to function properly. As it is in the natural, so it is in the spiritual. Each part of the ear has an important role, like the **Pinna,** which collects the sound waves, while the **oval window** facilitates movements, and it's also the membrane covering the entrance to the inner ear. Impulses, sound and balance to the brain is carried by the **auditory nerve**, while the three semicircular **canal** contains fluid which helps us to keep our balance. Each little part plays a vital role, and without some of them our brain will either be oblivious (not aware /concerned) to the noise around us or we lose our physical balance.

Why did Apostle Paul use analogies of the natural body parts to ask questions?

Do we see the rhythm and vital importance of every body part? Isaiah 30:21- *"And thy ears shall hear a word behind thee, saying, This is the way, walk ye in it, when ye turn to the right hand, and when ye turn to the left."*

*"My sheep hears my voice, and I know them, and they follow me"* John 10:27.

Revelation 2:29, *"He that hath an ear, let him hear what the Spirit saith unto the Churches."*

Repeatedly, the word of the Lord encourages the believer about the importance of 'hearing with the ear.'

## Reflections

Let us appreciate our natural healthy ears and those placed in the spiritual body to listen and declare confirmation of Elohim's words by his Spirit. We need all the parts of the ear to be appreciated, come in alignment to function in the structures. Let us not stubbornly or presumptuously ignore the importance of the hearing ear.

## Prayer

Forgive us heavenly Father for ignoring the detail

instruction we hear, and let us be sensitive to listen and obey Your Spirit to treat the ear with importance.

Chapter 6

# FOR THE BODY IS NOT ONE MEMBER BUT MANY PARTS 4
*Memory Verse: I Corinthians 12:17*

*"If the whole body were an eye, where were the hearing? If the whole were hearing, where were the smelling?"*
The eye of the body facilitates light and balance both in the natural and in the spiritual. It is emphatic to even imagine the whole body as the eye. There are about eighteen structures of the anatomy of the eye. To list just a few would limit each part of the eye's capacity, as each part is important to the functionality to see.

The external eye muscle moves the eyeball, the sclera is the tough protective layer (white of the eye) which provides protection. The **choroid** supplies the capillaries with nutrients. The **cornea** is the transparent window, and acts as the eye's most important lens. It controls and focuses the entry of light into the eye. **Aqueous humor** is the clear watery fluid between the cornea and the front of the vitreous. It bathes the eye, nourishes the lens and cornea which have no blood supply. It performs the blood's job for carrying nutrients to those structures, helps the eyeball keep its shape. The **Lens** helps to focus light on the retina. The suspensory ligament support the lens. The **lachrymal gland** manufacture tears. The **ciliary muscle** contracts and relaxes to alter the shape of the lens. The **retina** converts light energy and nerve impulses. The **optic nerve** transmits nerve impulses to the brain. The **blind spot** has no retina, no vision at this point. The **yellow spot** provides detail vision at the center cones of the eyes only. The **pupil** is the entrance or hole which light passes. The **Iris** controls the amount of light through the pupil.

Can we see the chain of command, unity, and the rhythm of the structures and function of the organ of the eye? How important are your eyes in the body? How do you treat your eyes?

## Reflection:

Let us be thankful for all the parts that allows the eye to function. If one part is sick or affected, it throws the complete eye out of balance and rhythm with its natural ability to function. If our light goes dim in the body, we are thrown off balance too.

While we sleep, our eyelids close voluntarily from the unique rhythm of how Elohim created and placed our eyeballs in sacs or cavities(space). When we wake in the morning, our eyes are coordinating with our brain/ mind as it's being renewed in the freshness of the word.

The nervous system is in alignment working in perfect unison. Our heavenly Father's eyes are watching over the universe and His children as in Psalm 32:8
*"I will instruct thee and teach you in the way which you shall go. I will counsel you, I will guide thee with my eye."*
We are uniquely and divinely place in Your Body for kingdom authority, building up each other in the most holy faith.

Matthew 6:22 & 23 *"The light of the body is the eye: if therefore thine eye be single; thy whole body shall be full of light. But if thine eye be evil, thy whole body shall be full of darkness, how great is that darkness!"*

**Prayer**

Father we thank you for 20/20 vision in the natural and in the spiritual realms. We thank you for healthy eyes and the strength in the muscles. We bless you for enhancing our body with the light of the eye that complements our balance and rhythm with movements.

We are grateful you have placed the eyes where they belong and could not otherwise be misplaced. We thank you for those who are gifted to see beyond what the physical eyes can detect and reveal your plans to the body to sustain us in times of adversity. We thank you for the confirmation of your word in Job 39:29, *"From thence she seeketh the prey. And her eyes behold it afar off"*.

Chapter 7

# FOR THE BODY IS NOT ONE MEMBER BUT MANY PARTS 5

*Memory Verse: I Corinthians 12:20*

*"But now are there many members, yet but one body."*
We celebrate in the uniqueness of our body parts. We are diverse and complex, sharing in the structures and functions of the oneness. We are essential and important workers together. 2 Corinthians 5: 20 says, *"Now then we are ambassadors for Christ, as though God did beseech you by us: we pray you in Christ's stead, be ye reconciled to God."*

As kingdom citizens, transforming into the image and likeness of Christ. We are admonished and exhorted that we should be growing into maturity. We cannot stay at the same level on milk like newborn babes. We need strong meat; our physical and spiritual nutrition should consist of a diet rich in essential nutrients to develop our body parts.

Without proper nutrition we are weak and sickly. Our immune system will deteriorate under any slight adverse circumstances of physical and spiritual life.
One member should not be fed, while the other parts are left malnourished. 2 Corinthians 6:1, *"We then, as workers together with him, beseech you also that ye receive not the grace of God in vain."* Verse 3, *"Giving no offense in anything that the ministry be not blamed."*

Often time in our natural diet we tend to eat things that are not wholesome to the body system, we either experience indigestion, gas reflux, diarrhea, vomiting, headaches, or constipation just to name a few signs and symptoms of some food that does not agree with our metabolism.

When we quickly adjust our diet, the body gradually heals itself. We can poison our own selves with things that are not conducive to the benefit of the body.

**Reflections:**
We can either accept or reject the laws and principles that are reality of the Creators agenda for our natural

and spiritual body, or face the consequences and repercussions.

**Prayers:**
May you filter us Lord Jesus and cleanse us by the washing of water and the word. Purify us by Your Spirit from all unrighteousness. Help us to understand the performance of our natural body parts. To get acquainted, and to discern the things of the Spirit, and how we fit in your Kingdom as citizens of heaven in Jesus Name we pray. Amen!

Romans 12: 4-5, Verse 4: *"For as we have many members in one body, and all the members have not the same office,"* Verse 5: *"Prophecy, let us prophesy according to the proportion of faith; Verse 6: Or he that exhorteth, on exhortation: let him do it with simplicity; he that ruleth, with diligence; he that sheweth mercy, with cheerfulness."*

Chapter 8

# POWER OF UNITY

*Memory Verse: I Corinthians 12:18*

*"But now hath God set the members every one of them in the body, as it pleased him."*

The Creator of the ends of the earth. The Alpha and Omega, The Ancient of Days does all things perfectly for his good pleasure.

Human coordination has shown us the purpose of unity and balance. We see clearly that we all need each other and are not to overlook or to despise another body part, as it goes against the laws of divinity meeting humanity.
For emphasis, we do not nourish one body part over the other. When we ingest food it goes into the stomach. The Food bag or gut process, breaks it down and it's distributed evenly in the blood stream to keep life going. The blood is important as the oxygen we inhale and

exhale. One cannot survive without the other. The heart needs all its valves in the four chambers to channel or pump the blood; it also depends on the respiratory system (lung). The Kidneys know its value and worth; cleansing the blood of toxin/poisons and transform the waste to urine. The kidneys are unique, bean shape and structure on either side of our spine. No other organ matches the looks, shape and size of the kidneys which are designed to do that function. Each kidney weighs about 160 grams. They eliminate up to one and a half liters of urine daily. The two kidneys working together filter 200 liters of fluid every 24 hours. I think of how Elohim formed the man Adam, took a rib from his side to create the woman Eve. Kidneys work side by side inside the body. They are described as a pair, like a husband and wife.

The head cannot function without the neck, the neck is attached to the shoulder bones, then the trunk of the body, and all our extremities are in their proper place. The internal organs cannot stay in place without the rib cage. The skeleton structure and skin are like guard rails covering and protecting the internal organs.

**Reflections.**
Like the natural body, all parts are all working together in unity for one common goal, keep life going daily. Each system within the body gives support to the others. Just the same in the spirit, each person's talent, gift and office in the body works together in unity to build up his kingdom.

**Prayer**
Loving Father and Creator: Thank You for thinking about us for your creation. For placing us all uniquely to serve in unison and not in competition but competing for the common goal, to be blessings to each other and bring glory to You Abba Father.

Thank You Father, Son and Holy Spirit that you show us unity in the kingdom of righteousness. You desire us to manifest unity generally in our everyday physical and spiritual nutrition.

Chapter 9

# EVERY BODY PART IS IMPORTANT
*Memory Verse: I Corinthians 12:19*

*"And if they were all one member, where were the body?"*

Paul asked this complex question to challenge our thinking. Complication manifest itself in chaos.
This is like reflecting on Genesis 1:2, *"And the earth was without form and void; and darkness was upon the face of the deep. And the Spirit of God-Elohim moved upon the face of the waters."* We would not exist as human beings to answer such a question.

Paul was addressing the chaos within the community of believers who, were showing partiality and favouritism. He exposes the reality of human behavior, and how we tend to place high value on those humans we feel are gifted while excluding others.

We should not see only dominant gifts, and ignore persons we think are of lesser value to our ministerial calling. We should not only esteem those persons we think are highly gifted, and sideline those we see as insignificant. The latter refers to those that Paul called 'the uncommonly parts'. Let us reason this in line with the natural functioning of our body parts. Do we neglect any of our body parts?

**Reflections:**
Everybody part is important. Would we have leaders without followers?

Men religiously create a pulpit so he could have a pew. Why not maintain attention to the pew only? It's not possible to have an audience without people and be the only one to function. Paul was addressing the selfishness of people's carnal thinking and lack of love and compassion.

**Prayer:**
Heavenly Father, may we, by Your Holy Spirit, embrace each other's significance in every Christian community. May we understand why You sent Jesus Christ/Yeshua

Hamashiac to redeem us. If You were only thinking about Yourself alone, you would not have us into Your creation. You thought of the body of Christ you called Your bride. Help us to be filled with the fruit of Your Spirit and manifest the fruits in our daily lives in Jesus Christ Name we thank you.

Chapter 10

# WHAT IS YOUR PURPOSE?
*Memory Verse: I Corinthians 12:21-22*

*"And the eye cannot say unto the hand, I have no need of thee: nor again the head to the feet, I have no need of you. Nay, much more those members of the body, which seem to be more feeble, are necessary."*

We need our eyes importantly as we walk, we gain light and balance. No one would deliberately pluck his eyes out because he feels it is not important. We need our hands to serve our own selves and others. We need our feet to move about.

The purpose of the hand, to be productive, show kindness, embrace each other, clap, and use to worship and praise Yahweh. These are placed strategically at our side to extend healing, to write, scratch our backs, reach for things, and so on.

Here we again decide to accept each body part as vital and important yet, in the spiritual kingdom we experience the short comings of how we treat others.

We are all unique, but sometimes might feel more important than others, especially when we are spotlighted or elevated to a position. We then go around, proud and puffed up, with an egocentric mentality, "It is me, myself and I."

May we come to the God consciousness that we need each other, and the spiritual kingdom is all about giving glory to the heavenly Father and serving each other. Let us be a blessing that the father can be pleased, in the spirit of humility and meekness, knowing we were once alienated but you have drawn us to You by Your grace and Mercy.

Psalm 144: 1 says: *"Blessed be the Lord my strength, which teacheth my hands to war, and my fingers to fight."*
We observe the Psalmist King David giving thanks to Adonai, Jehovah Gibor for enabling his hands with strength to overcome his adversaries. It was with his hands he got empowerment to stretch and aim that slingshot at Goliath in the faith of Elohim. He conquered

a Bear and a Lion with those arms that were anointed by Yahweh. We need our hands in spiritual warfare as we raised them, as we clap, we are engaged in spiritual warfare.

The hands of the Lord is our hands in the earth doing great things on His behalf as we yield them to him. Our feet shod with the preparation of the gospel of peace. We need our hands, feet, our other eyes, to corporate, coordinate and work as a team in the kingdom of God. Let us draw closer to each other and show the father's Agape Love.

**Reflections:**
What would the organ of the eye be without a body or a hand? Paul used to question our thinking. He is challenging our abilities to think constructively about each member's importance and significance. Their purpose and capabilities and the things we were all created and born to do. He is giving us things to think about. The bigger picture of our purpose is living the transformed life as kingdom spiritual beings that we were ordained to be before the foundation of the world by Elohim-Adonai.

**Prayer**

Matthew 5:14, I am the light of the world. A city that is set on a hill cannot be hid. Neither do men light a candle, and put it under a bushel, but on a candlestick; and it giveth light unto all that are in the house.

Holy Spirit help me shine my light before men, that they may see your good works, and glorify the Father which is in heaven.

Isaiah 60:1 My soul Arise, shine for thy light is come, and the glory of the Lord is risen upon thee.

Chapter 11

# KNOWING THE PURPOSE OF THE ARMS AND HANDS 1
*Memory Verse: I Corinthians 12:21-22*

*"And the eye cannot say unto the hand, I have no need of thee: nor again the head to the feet, I have no need of you. Nay, much more those members of the body, which seem to be more feeble, are necessary."*

How important for the eye and the hand to coordinate with purpose? Isaiah 41: 13 & 15, *"For I the Lord thy God will hold thy right hand, saying unto thee, Fear not; I will help."* Verse 15 *"Behold, I will make thee a new sharp threshing instrument having teeth: thou shalt thresh the mountains, and beat them small, and shalt make the hills as chaff."*

With the same hands, Elohim anointed him to slay Goliath with a sling and stone. His fingers were necessary on his hands. Every digit were strengthened by Jehovah Gibor. He explained when a Lion and Bear came to attack the sheep, he tore them to pieces.

There is something about the hand that holds the shield of faith and the sword of the Spirit. There is something about the hand of the five wise virgins who took their oil and preserved it for the call of the bridegroom.
Matthew 25:1-13, The seeing eye, the hearing ear and the hands are spiritual analogy descriptive of the events of the virgins awaiting the bridegroom. They were actively watching, waiting, and listening.

We see the Five-fold Ministry playing its administrative role in the structures and function of the Bride of Christ. The Spiritual Kingdom is well equipped to rule and reign from a heavenly perspective in the earth.

**Prayer**
We thank You Almighty God, for you have made us all important and we are all unique in his eyes.

Chapter 12

# KNOWING THE PURPOSE OF THE ARMS AND HANDS 2

*Memory Verse: I Corinthians 12:23,24,25, 26 & 27*

*"And those members of the body which we think to be less honorable, upon these we bestow more abundant honor, and our uncomely parts have more abundant comeliness."* For our comely parts have no need, but God hath tempered the body together, having given more abundant honor to that part which lacked: That there should be no schism in the body, but that the members should have the same care one for another.

And whether one member suffer, all the members suffer with it; or one member be honored, all the members rejoice with it. Now ye are the body of Christ, and members in particular. We tend to go for the outward appearances, the masculine beauty, the feminine beauty, the adornment of fancy apparels.

## Example of James chapter 2:1-10

*"My brethren have not faith of our Lord Jesus Christ, the Lord of Glory, with respect of persons. For if there come unto your assembly a man with a gold ring, in goodly apparel, and there come in a poor man in vile raiment. And ye have respect to him that weareth the gay clothing, and say unto him, sit thou here in a good place, and say to the poor, stand thou here, or sit here under my footstool: Are ye not partial in yourselves, and are become judges of evil thoughts? Hearken, my beloved brethren, hath God chosen the poor of this world rich in faith, and heirs of the kingdom which he hath promised to them that love him?*

*But ye have despised the poor. Do not rich men oppress you, and draw you before the judgement seats?*

*But if ye have respect to persons, ye commit sin, and are convinced of the law, and yet offend in one point, he is guilty of all.*

## Reflections:

While we are impressed by the outward appearances within the body, Jehovah is seeking the heart. Rend your heart and not your garments.

The same people that cried out hosanna, were the same people crying out, give us Barabbas and crucify him! *"These people draw near to Me with their mouth... But their heart is far from Me."* Matthew 15:8.

We see the bias and bureaucracy within the body that cause the partiality. The little foxes on the vine that causes distractions from the true purposes of the Kingdom.

**Prayer**
May we draw near with broken and contrite hearts, ready and willing to embrace unity and peace. Lord help us avoid discord but choose divine wisdom.

## Chapter 13

# CARE FOR ONE ANOTHER
*Memory Verse: I Corinthians 12:24-25*

*"For our comely parts have no need: but God hath tempered the body together, having given more abundant honor to that part which lacked. That there should be no schism in the body; but that the members should have the same care one for another."*

God desires us to be radiant on the inside and take care of our temple. Looking good and attractive is temporal, we should be lovely and take pride in our natural appearances as his vessels of honor. However, He is more interested on what goes on in our inner man.

Are we walking in love and being our brother's keeper? Do we care for one another? God desire us to develop love and sensitivity for each other. Our care for each other is important in the community. Are we concerned when a member is out of a job or unemployed? How do we offer our emotional and moral support to others?

Galatians 6: 9-10, *"And let us not be weary in well doing for in due season we shall reap, if we faint not. As we have opportunity, let us do good unto all men, especially unto them who are of the household of faith."*

Romans 12:13, Distributing to the necessity of the saints; given to hospitality.

James chapter 2:14,15, 16 & 26
James chapter1:27
*"Pure religion and undefiled before God and the Father is this, to visit the fatherless and widows in their affliction, and to keep himself unspotted from the world."*

## Reflections:

When one body part hurts the entire body experience the repercussion or impact of discomfort, pain, or dislocation.

I remember experiencing a fungus under my fingernail (cuticle). I tried treating it with different home remedies and it seem to get worst until I discovered the natural antibiotic in garlic. I crushed a peg of garlic and administered it one night to the nail with a piece of gauze.

That night I felt my entire nervous system was sensitive to the throbbing as the garlic penetrated the bacteria. I felt a sharp pain, as if an injection needle was stuck in my flesh. I was in agony from the pain in that little finger. I resisted removing the garlic treatment but groaned loudly, trying to fall asleep. The pain was excruciating, and to think it was just a tiny body part.

**Prayer:**
Heavenly Father, you send the Lord Jesus, who is our living Christ that send his Holy Spirit to live within us. Help us to be more tolerant and sensitive to each other needs and care for them. You have not called us to unnecessary burdens but to help alleviate another's discomfort in whatever way we can as we listen to your heart and instructions. You give us strategies and creative ideas that can intervene in many situations. Help us to know your voice and obey your commands and promptings.

We thank you for your righteousness, joy, and peace in the Holy Spirit, which is in Your kingdom.
Amen. Amen. Amen.

Chapter 14

# THE DIFFERENT MINISTERIAL GIFTS PART 1

*Memory Verse: I Corinthians 12:27-28*

*"And God hath set some in the Church, first Apostles, secondarily prophets, thirdly teachers, after that miracles, then gifts of healings, helps, governments, diversities of tongues."*

Here we read and see the lay out of the five-fold ministerial gifting or callings endowed by the Holy Spirit within the Church, the Body of Christ.

We can use our five fingers to remember the five-fold ministry offices. Here again we see the natural body part enhancing and complimenting the spiritual kingdom.

- The thumb represents the Apostle's office; he is a church planter and embraces other local assemblies, signs and wonder should follow his ministerial calling like the

Apostle Paul.

- The index finger represents the prophet; points the way forward. He is a Seer, operates in the word of wisdom and word of knowledge. Confirming what God has already promised. Example of Jeremiah called from the womb.

- The middle finger represents the call of the evangelist (Philip was mentioned as an Evangelist). The individual in this office is fiery, passionately burdened for souls and always witnessing to the unsaved and backsliders.

- The ring finger represents love, care; the pastor or Shepherd of the flock. He is a nurturer. He is stationed within an assembly to guard, teach, encourage, guide, exhort, and counsel. Though he might go by invitation or travel out, he has a set group or congregation to oversee.

- We focus now on the 'pinky' little finger, the teacher of the word. Uniquely chosen to be tiny, so to add flexibility. He or she is passionate for details, and digs deep in the word. They stir deep in the soil of the word for hidden truths (gems, pearls of great price) They break down and deliver the word that others may have found difficult to understand, like the Messiah- Jesus Christ himself was the greatest teacher of all using nature, and everyday experience to bring his message across. A teacher inspires and motivates in his presentation of the word. He studies intensely and will find the pearl of great price that we tend to overlook in each verse, passage, or paragraph.

Example: Isaiah 28:9-10, *"Whom shall he teach knowledge? And whom shall he make to understand doctrine? Them that are weaned from the milk and drawn from the breast. For precept must be upon precept, precept upon precept; line upon line, line upon; here a little, and there a little:"* The teacher is diverse and creative is aspect of bringing out artistic insights.

The responsibilities of the teaching and pastoral ministry is to present the word accurately not based on intellectual or theologically training and ability, but the inspiration of the Holy Spirit: Spiritual things are spiritually discerned as apostle Paul stated in: 1 Corinthians chapter 2: 1-16 verse 9-12 *"But as it is written, Eye hath not seen, nor ear heard, neither have entered into the heart of man, the things which God hath prepared for them that love him. But God hath revealed them unto us by his Spirit: for the Spirit searcheth all things, yea, the deep things of God. For what man knoweth the things of a man, save the spirit of man which is in him? Even so the things of God knoweth no man, but the Spirit of God.*

*Now we have received, not the spirit of the world, but the spirit is of God; that we might know the things that are freely given to us of God."*

Here the Apostle emphasized the most important person in a believer's life is to be endued by the Holy Sprit's help to deliver the words of truths.

**Prayer:**
Lord help me to use the gift you have given me to be a blessing. Let my words transform lives and bring hope.

Chapter 15

# THE DIFFERENT MINISTERIAL GIFTS PART 2

*Memory Verse: Ephesians 4:6-8*

Scripture says that when Jesus the Messiah ascended to heaven he gave gifts to men, and also the grace to accomplish these gifts. *There is one body, and one Spirit, even as ye are called in one hope of your calling; One Lord, one faith, one baptism. One God and Father of all, who is above all, and through all, and in you all. But unto every one of us is given grace according to the measure of the gift of Chris*t.

We have the different gifts given to individuals by the Holy Spirit like, the Word of knowledge, Faith, Prophecy, Healing, Miracles, Discernment Of Spirits, Diverse Tongues & Interpretation. All of which main purpose is to edify/build up the Church. We shall delve deeper into a few.

**The Gift of Healing:** This is a supernatural ability to deliver different types of healing, and restoration of health. Acts 19:11, Luke 4:40, Luke 25: 5, Mark 10:16 Mark 16:18.

**The Gift of Miracles** can at times intertwine with the healing ministry where a body part can supernaturally grow out. Blind eyes restored; deaf ears open, dead raised, to name a few. As well as changing the weather, moving the cause of natural elements, like the parting of the Red Sea, Jesus turning water into wine, and the multiplication of the five loaves and two fishes.

**The Gift of Administration** - the gift to keep things ordered and in agreement with God's principles.
The Gift of Help This area within many local Assembly is often neglected or despised. Some people's preference would be preaching from a pulpit, and would think they are not called to exercise menial work. Let us take into consideration that if many of us were not serving at this level what would happen to cleanliness and proper environmental sanitation?

A servant whose heart is passionate about hospitality, serving people is also indirectly witnessing the heart of Jesus Christ. Our action should manifest loving compassion and kindness like Jesus the Messiah.

**Reflections:**

To grow in our spiritual gifts, we need to allow the word of God to take root in our lives. It teaches us who we are in Christ, and know our worth is not based on position or titles. Elohim wants us whole and complete in him. He must get His bride ready for his glorious appearing without spots or wrinkle. He is faithful and true to his promises. The God of All creation was a great example when he took a towel, stooped down, and began washing his disciples' feet. John 13:5-20, Verse 16 & 17 *"Verily, verily, I say unto you, The servant is not greater than his Lord; neither he that is sent greater than he that sent him. If ye know these things, happy are ye if ye do them."*

1 Peter 4:10 *"Each of you should use whatever gift you have received to serve others, as faithful stewards of God's grace in its various forms."* We are all called to serve in humility. There is no big or small. To do this we all need to get down from any high horse, reject foolish pride, and serve at the bottom of the ladder. Many capitalize on being served, but lack the humility to serve others. The scripture charges us to serve as faithful steward and not

be proud and puffed up.

James 4:6 But He gives more grace. Therefore it says, *"God opposes the proud, but gives grace to the humble."* We need to remember it is by His grace that we are, not by our own strength. If we bear this key thing in mind, it will make us more effective to serve with love.

Let us take a note from the life of Samson. After the philistines shaved his hair, he rose up and shook himself thinking he was still in his own strength not realizing the Spirit of God had departed from him.

Chapter 16

# THE DIFFERENT MINISTERIAL GIFTS PART 3

*Memory Verse: 1 Corinthians 12:28*

*"And God hath set some in the Church, first Apostles, secondarily prophets, thirdly teachers, after that miracles, then gifts of healings, helps, governments, diversities of tongues."*

**The Gift of Government/Administration:** This gift bring order and organisation according to God's plan. Isaiah 9:6, *"For unto us a child is born, unto us a son is given, and the government shall be upon his shoulder: and his name shall be called Wonderful, Counselor, The Mighty God, The Everlasting Father, The Prince of Peace."*

The Church has been mandated to be organized, structured under the Holy Spirit supervision. There is authority given to us to maintain wholesome administration as body of believers, to have dominion in the earth realm. We are called to be a spiritual advisor and educator to the world system. A replica of the kingdom of God and His authority on earth.

Paul admonishes in 1 Timothy chapter 2: 1-8, The responsibility of the Church government ensure firstly that supplications, prayers, intercession and giving of thanks, be made for all men. For kings, and for all that is in authority; that we may lead a quiet and peaceable life in all godliness and honesty.

When we read down to the other verses, it charges us, the body of Christ to stand as mediators and decree and declare heaven's Lordship on earth. The church as an institution in the earth has the authority to bind and loose. To shift anything that is not in alignment with the governance of Jehovah's principles and protocols… As in heaven let it be in the earth.

The agreement prayer should be reinforced by the church government. We should never miss a rhythm of a beat to stand as God's oracles and command righteous judgements to superimpose any other unrighteousness. We pray His Kingdom come on earth as it is in heaven, Mathew 6:8.

The Church Government in the nation is significant and relevant to represents the throne room of heaven.

The first Adam had lost dominion in the garden of Eden. Jesus Christ became our second Adam and gave the Church back dominion and a mandate to follow a pattern, a model of authority. He told Peter; *"Upon this rock I build my Church and the gates of hell shall not prevail against it."*

Matthew 6:9-13; The model Prayer

*"After this manner therefore pray ye: Our Father, who art in heaven, Hallowed be thy Name, thy Kingdom come on earth as it is in heaven. Give us this day our daily bread. And forgive us our debts, as we forgive our debtors. And lead us not into temptation, but deliver us from all evil: For thine is the kingdom, and the power, and the glory, for ever and ever, Amen."*

I grew up saying this prayer repetitively and religiously, however, there are revelations and freshness to this decree and declarations.

We should use his words to build on it. Following the principles and protocols to understand why we pray or communicate with the Alpha, Omega (he is the beginning of all things and the ending of all things. He can shut down the cosmos as he pleases.

## Reflections

Acknowledge the great and mighty deity that is above all. He is Holy (consecrated, greatly reverence, sacred, recognizable above all gods that are useless) and his name must be highly honored. His kingdom is in us on the earth just as he operates in heaven, we have his authority to activate His will spiritually on earth. He is omnipresence, he is everywhere at the same time. Omniscience, he is all knowing, He has a kingdom, he has the power (omnipotent - unlimited power) all glory- magnificence, honor, great beauty, excellence, belongs to him, and we share in such attributes.

## Prayer

Lord we thank you that you are the source of all we need daily. Teach us to live in forgiveness towards each other as we seek your forgiveness. We trust in your faithfulness, and have confidence that you will protect us from all evil.

Chapter 17

# DIVERSITIES OF TONGUES

*Memory Verse: 1 Corinthians 12:28*

*"And God hath set some in the Church, first Apostles, secondarily prophets, thirdly teachers, after that miracles, then gifts of healings, helps, governments, diversities of tongues."*

We have been equipped by the power of the Holy Spirit, with supernatural heavenly languages.
Romans 8: 27, *"And he who searches our hearts knows the mind of the Spirit, because the Spirit intercedes for God's people in accordance with the will of God."*
As a faith believer I discovered when praying for a particular issue in english or any other language lacked the right vocabulary. I sometimes would start decreeing scriptures and yield my tongue to the Holy Spirit. He takes over praying through me supernaturally.

Often times I will be singing, and my tongue begins to give utterance in other languages. Awesome God! He is supernatural and He is Spirit! The Holy Spirit also gives me the interpretation in english. I have written the interpretation of worship songs as the Holy Spirit enabled my understanding.

Once at my dad's prayer center. A young sister, in my age group was troubled by the devil. We decided to have her stay with us while we ministered to her. That day in the prayer center as I was worshiping in my prayer language, I heard her distinctly making utterances and my daddy took authority over that foul spirit and it stopped speaking through her. Then it became clear to me how Satan also counterfeits the gift of tongues.

Many times, while around individuals from other cultures, I am at awe as I keenly listen to the different dialect and watch as their words are formed and roll off their tongues. God in his infinite plans for creation arranged all languages to be so unique. Many times, I question if our prayer language is not similar to another culture's dialect. It is amazing how the supernatural is divinely orchestrated by such an infallible: Deity-great and mighty Elohim.

1 Corinthians 14:15, *"What is it then? I will pray with the spirit, and I will pray with the understanding also: I will sing with the spirit, and I will sing with the understanding."* There is this rhythm and balance with the human spirit connecting with the Holy Spirit. We experience this being endowed with the Spirit's empowerment.

Our spirit yielding to the Holy Spirit becomes effective with supernatural diversities of heavenly languages. We were created firstly to be spiritual beings. Our spirit-man gets saved first when we repent from our sins and accept the Lord Jesus Christ into our lives, complemented by water baptism by immersion.

Ephesians 6:18, *"Praying always with all prayers and supplication in the Spirit and watching thereunto with all perseverance and supplication for all saints."* Our natural body and soul would be overwhelmed and burdened physically with this instruction without the help of the Holy Spirit. How could we pray always without the capacity of the Holy Spirit? Praying in the Spirit shows flexibility as a multitasking assignment. As we engage in different chores or duties, we can still pray without going aside to kneel, sit, prostrate or bow religiously,.

We can be praying under our breath quietly as we move around. Internally, we keep communing through our spirit. The Holy Spirit is uniquely strategized to enable us keep the communion going.

Romans 8:25, *"Likewise, the Spirit also helpeth our infirmities: for we know not we should pray for as we ought: but the Spirit itself maketh intercession for us with groanings which cannot be uttered."*
**Groanings:** A deep travail, moaning or groaning often supernaturally endowed in the inner heart of the believer while praying. It goes on deep down in the womb of his or her spirit, void of expression or utterances in verbal words. The Spirit beareth witness with our spirit, that we are the children of God.

John 14:26, *"But the Comforter, which is the Holy Ghost, whom the Father will send in my name, he shall teach you all things, and bring all things to your remembrance, whatsoever I have said unto you."* He promised us a part of him to live inside of us and to be our paraclete (helper). He assists us in all our weaknesses. He is our enabler.

Acts 2: 1-4, This *Reveals the manifestation of the promise of the Holy Spirit. *

… And they were all filled with the Holy Ghost and began to speak with other tongues as the Spirit gave them utterance.

Joel chapter 2 reveals by Peter in, verse 17: *"And it shall come to pass in the last days, saith God, I will pour out of my Spirit upon all flesh: and your sons and daughters shall prophesy, and your young men shall see visions, and your old men shall dream dreams."* Verse 18: And on my servants and on my handmaidens, I will pour out in those days of my Spirit; and they shall prophesy:

Was this scripture made evident as the Messiah Jesus Christ spoke in tongues on the cross?

Mark 15: 34, *"And at the ninth hour Jesus cried with a loud voice, saying, Eloi, Eloi, lama sabachtham? Which is being interpreted, My God, my God, Why hast thou forsaken me? It was a language that many mentioned he was calling for Elias."*

My reasoning and question is, many could not attest (proven or have a clear evidence) that it was a native language they knew? Reference to speaking in tongues of men and of Angels: 1 Corinthians 13:1 "Though I speak with tongues of men and of angels and have not charity (love) I become as a sounding brass or a tinkling symbol. 1 Corinthians 14:1-33, Paul addresses the gift of speaking in tongues: Summary of his explanations: Crave after agape love, however, desire spiritual gifts. Most importantly, crave for the gift of prophecy, which brings edification and confirmation of God's plans, truths for the future and encouragements. This gift is like a road map or guide for us as individuals to stay in the course of the will of God for us as individual saints and the general assembly/church body to stay focused from distractions. As our tongues continue supernaturally in communication with God in realms of the Spirit, He (God) understands perfectly the mysteries.

Prophecy reveals the heart of God by his Spirit to us his saints. Those things that the Holy Spirit chose to allow an individual to discern in the spiritual realm through word of knowledge, word of wisdom and the gift of discernment, He enables the seer to explain and deliver this revelation. As Paul went on to say, that he desires that we speak in our heavenly languages, but importantly, we should flow in the prophetic; this is greater, to edify, and to build up the church.

No matter how I flow in the gift of tongues, if I am giving thanks to God, others will not know because there's no interpretation. If it is a word for edification for others the gift of interpretation will manifest. Paul explains how musical instruments like the harp, the flute and the piano, give distinct sounds that we all can be familiar with. In essence, if we receive the utterances of tongues we also have been given, the ability by the Holy Spirit to easily interpret. If this does not happen, no one will be able to understand and we are speaking just to the wind. He emphasized that there are so many voices in the world, and they all have significance.

If I am ignorant (not aware, or literate) of the voice, I am to that person, a foreigner/ alien to the other person language and vice versa. He advised us, that though we have zeal (enthusiasm, motivation, energized or gusto), seek to be excellent in the Spirit to edify, encourage, build up or encourage the saints. He went on to explain his personal experiences: his spirit prays but his understanding is unfruitful.

I have similar experiences, where I have been hurt badly by individual/s and I would be praying on such issues, sometimes I start to sob uncontrollably, then supernatural heavenly languages begin to roll off my tongue which I cannot express or describe. It flows just like a river. I may not get an interpretation; however, I would feel so relieved and refreshed in his presence.

On another occasion in a general assembly, an evangelist ministered under the prophetic to me concerning my writings. As he ministered, I felt the confirmation deep down in my spirit. As I bowed down, worshiping in tongues I felt His supernatural presence. Later, someone came and embraced me, and immediately I felt in my spirit that the person was stifling my spirit and the prophetic word that was given. I then went on the floor worshiping; suddenly, I felt my spirit transition into deep warfare in tongues.

The Holy Spirit is an intelligent deity. Even when we are drunk in the Spirit, and at times the physical body is weakened by his awesome presence, in his manifestation, he allows our spirit to be sober and alert. How can the unlearned who has no clue of the spiritual things confirm what is said in tongues? I am edified in my spirit man uniting with the Holy Spirit, but others are not edified or encouraged.

Paul in essence was not boastful or bragging, he was just expressing his own personal relationship for clarification. *"I thank my God; I speak in tongues more that ye all."* 1 Corinthians 14:18. Paul personally gave honor to the most High first. He shifts his focus to the body of Christ: He encouraged that we should not behave petty or foolish but be sober in the spirit. Avoid childish behavior, as if we are using our tongues for a show.

*"Therefore tongues are for a sign, not to those who believe but to unbelievers; but prophesying is not for unbelievers but for those who believe."* 1 Corinthians 14:22.
God uses the Prophetic to expose hidden truths, whether of sin or righteousness. This gift affects holy fear and reverence along with the gift of discernment. Many will come to repentance when their secrets are revealed and exposed. In verse 28: We see here the great admonition of rhythm and balance to bring order and usefulness to all members in the body. Everyone should have something deposited by the Spirit in their vessels: A hymn, a Psalm, a doctrine, a tongue, a revelation, interpretation, Let all be to the encouragement of the whole body of Christ.

Here we see the structures and function of many body parts participating. Church government and administration is advised in verses 27-33, God is no author of Confusion: If he has order in heaven, there must be order in his body, the bride of Christ. The natural body has order and every part and system are structured to function in order. When one is out of order. Something abnormal is occurring. So, in the physical body, so in the spiritual body.

**Reflections:**

Though I am empowered, equipped and supernaturally given the gift of tongues, if I am not manifesting his sincere agape love, I am not manifesting the fruit in the Spirit. I can be functioning in lawlessness (iniquity). Matthew 6: 15 *"Ye shall know them by their fruits. Do men gather grapes of thorns, or figs of thistles?"*

*"Not everyone that saith unto me Lord, Lord, shall enter into the kingdom of heaven; but he that doeth the will of my Father which is in heaven."* Matthew 7:21. So, we can be so caught up doing ministry, fulfilling religious duties, and still not doing the will of the heavenly Father.

Verse 22: *"Many will say in that day, Lord, Lord, have we not prophesied in thy name? And in thy name cast out devils? And in thy name done many wonderful works? And then I will profess unto them, I never knew you; depart from me ye workers of iniquity."*

Working the gifts without repentance, using manipulation (witchcraft and disobedience) God's anointing is no more on the person's life. He has left the place of his grace. His agape love, mercy and grace is no more there.

**Prayer**
Heavenly Father, Thank You for sending your only begotten son as the Messiah: Yeshua Hamashiach, our Lord and Savior Jesus Christ and for him sending the Holy Spirit as our Comforter, teacher who guides us into all truths and brings all things to our remembrance.

Thank You for His indwelling inside of us as we yield to him and acknowledge him as our enabler or helper. Thank You for his manifested presence and the gifts of tongues and interpretation. Thank you, for we are graced with heavenly languages. Let us be transformed and manifest your agape love. As he enables us to communicate in diverse tongues, we live better lives daily to please you and be blessings to our fellow mankind, in Jesus mighty name, Amen!

Chapter 18

# BEING EFFECTIVE IN OUR GIFTS

*Memory Verse: 1 Corinthians 12:28*

*"And God hath set some in the Church, first Apostles, secondarily prophets, thirdly teachers, after that miracles, then gifts of healings, helps, governments, diversities of tongues."*

What statement are we making to the outside world by how we serve inside His kingdom?
2 Corinthians 5:20, *"Now then we are ambassadors for Christ, as though God did beseech you by us: we pray you in Christ's stead, be ye reconciled to God."*
1 Corinthians 3:9, *"For we are laborers together with God: ye are God's husbandry, ye are God's building."*
We read about the patriarchs and prophets and the different strategic positions they served in. Do we realize that while many of them were serving the heathen in Babylon, they represented their faith in Elohim?

How do we serve our widows, orphans, destitute, what provisions are many of us as kingdom citizens arranging for them? James 1:26-27, *"If any man among you seem to be religious, and bridleth not his tongue, but deceiveth his own heart, this man's religion is vain. Pure religion and undefiled before God and the Father is this, To visit the fatherless and widows in their affliction, and to keep himself unspotted from the world."*

## Reflections:
Galatians 6:10, *"As we have therefore opportunity, let us do good unto all men, especially unto them who are of the household of faith."*
Romans 12:13, *"Distributing to the necessity of the saints given to hospitality."* God's heart towards his people, the Ecclesia, the called out ones are for us to evaluate our motives as kingdom Citizens. Are we going to continue to allow the cares of life to consume us, and we miss an opportunity with Him in eternity?

## Prayer:
Lord Jesus, when we ask you to make us more than an ordinary servant, let us be aware of the cost. We do not know the cost of the Oil in the Alabaster Box.

Chapter 19

# THE HOLY SPIRIT OUR HELPER

*Memory Verse: 1 Corinthians 12:29-30*

"Are all apostles? Are all prophets? Are all teachers? Are all workers of miracles? Have all the gifts of healing? Do all speak with tongues? Do all interpret? But covet earnestly the best gifts: and yet shew I unto you a more excellent way."

I could conclude by asking, are all body parts the same in the natural body? In the secular career field, do all specialize or function in the same specific job function? If every believer had the same calling and gifting, what would happen in a church community? It is extremely rewarding when we work to leave a mark, footprints, impacting our community, the nations, and the body of Christ.

However, if we at any time venture into something that we were not born to do or accomplish, our lives will not be happy. Doing something to gain man's approval will be a ruin to one's own sanity, because your life can be spent in misery, but when you find that niche where you know that you know you belong and are comfortable with, it eases stress and you are at peace.

Paul, asked the question about, *"...if all believers speak in tongues?"* Not all believers have been endowed with the gift of tongues, yet they have the Spirit of God. Instead, we should appreciate the fruit of the Spirit manifesting in their lives. (Galatians 5:22-23) We should concentrate more on the fruit bearing.

It is of vital necessity, and mandatory that the Spirit of the Living God have possession of our being. "The proof of the ingredients is in the pudding." However, he will not force himself if we do not allow him in. We have to make room for him so to speak.
Romans 8:8-9, *"So, then, they that are in the flesh cannot please God. But ye are not in the flesh, but in the Spirit, if so be that the Spirit of God dwell in you. Now, if any man have not the Spirit of Christ, he is none of his."* The Holy Spirit is our seal of promise. We have no unction to function well without him; just relying on head (theoretical) knowledge or intellectual training. There will be no

deep conviction or conversion without the experience and infilling of the Holy Spirit. He is the Anointing that moves upon the gifts and talents for effectiveness in a supernatural way.

**Prayer:**

Come as the refiner's fire Holy Spirit. Endue us with power from on high. Empower us, fill us, sustain us, refresh us. Fill us with the boldness and confidence we need as believers to live the persevering, enduring life of faith. When you come to live in us, you are our teacher, our guide, and our comforter. You will be in our mind and remind us of the heavenly promises, and bring all things to our memory in time of need. You will pray through us when we have inadequate or insufficient vocabulary. Help us to become more acquainted with You and the presence of the triune Elohim. We thank You for comforting us. Amen!

Chapter 20

# SUMMARY

*Memory Verse: Ephesians 2:21*

*In whom all the building fitly framed together groweth unto an holy temple in the Lord*

The Purpose the body of Christ is called to unity, is summed up in *Ephesians 2:20-22*, the great finale climax into Yahweh's Kingdom Agenda; *"20.And are built upon the foundation of the apostles and prophets, Jesus Christ himself being the chief corner stone. 21.In whom all the building fitly framed together groweth unto an holy temple in the Lord; 22.In whom ye are builded together for an habitation of God through the Spirit."*

Unity is the structure and function of the body of Christ. This can be seen in Ephesians chapter 1 through to chapter 4: 1-16, *"Till we all come in the unity of the (a) Faith, and of the knowledge of (b)* **Who?** *The Son of God.* \***Purpose**\*

*Perfect man, unto the measure of the stature of the fullness of Christ."*

*The Enable Body* is the embodiment of a risen Christ ushering us into oneness, completeness.

**Summary Highlights:**

Walk worthy of the vocation in which we are called.

The essential Fruit of the Spirit.

Unity and the bond of peace.

*One body. One Faith. One Baptism. *

One God and Father of all in Us All.

Everyone is given grace according to the measure of the gift of Christ.

He descended in humanity, laying aside his divinity.

He ascended in order to distribute the gifts.

He Emancipated/freed Zion!

He made Himself known far above all heavens, that he might fill or complete all things.

Summary

**Welcome to the Five -Fold Ministry Gifts!** The right hand of empowerment, an **Invitation to Unity.** Ephesians 4:11 states *"And He gave some: Apostles, and some, Prophets, and some, Evangelist, and some, Pastors, and Teachers;* **For:** *1. The perfecting of the saints 2. For the work of the Ministry 3. For the edifying of the body of Christ."*

**What is the Fullness of Christ?**

This is the foundation of His plans and purposes, which is His finished work on the cross. His mandate for his citizens is to be transformed in his image and likeness. Getting us back to the original plan/agenda of dominion and authority in his kingdom realm. Reigning with him for eternity.

His desire is that we are stable, sober, and of a sound mind, being confident in faith. We should not be easily swayed or seduced by deception of evil men(humanity) who are crooked, twisted, double minded, perverted. The traps or devices, snares are always there with enchantments to entice his sheep to stray, however, he placed his ministers to fit in place in their offices of administrations.

*The Enabled Body*, is a call to unity in Christ! **Unity must be mandatory in His agape-love.** Order must be established, The body of Christ needs to develop, grow, enlarge, and advance in all things. Above all, recognize the Sovereign headship intertwined with Christ. As Colossians 1:18 clearly states, *"And he is the head of the body, the church."*

Ephesians 4:16 states, *"From whom the whole body fitly joined together, and compacted by that which every joint supplieth, according to the effectual working in the measure of every part, maketh increase of the body unto the edifying of itself in love."*

A call to unity, is the birthing of His manifestation, Romans Chapter 8: 19, Creation is waiting for the manifestation of the sons of God.

Verse 22 *"For we know that the whole creation groaneth and travaileth in pain together until now. 23. Not only they, but ourselves also, which have the first fruits of the Spirit, even we ourselves groan within ourselves, waiting for the adoption, to wit, the redemption of our body."*

Are we not called the *new creation* of saints? Are we not a chosen generation, a royal priesthood, an holy nation, a peculiar people? 1 Peter2 :9.

*The Enabled Body* cries from the womb of the Spirit for unity, representative of the Bride of Christ, A call to unity in all her completeness.

May the whole chapters of Ephesians take root in our spirit-man, causing us to lay hold of our spiritual inheritance, our identity as kingdom citizens, awaiting to be adorned as the Bride of Christ, Yeshua Hamashiach.

*The Enabled Body* Cries from the womb of the Spirit for Unity. Isaiah 66:7-8, *"Before she travailed, she brought forth; before her pain came, She was delivered of a man child. 8. Who hath heard such things? Who hath seen such things? Shall the earth be made to bring forth in a day? Or shall a nation be born at once? For as Zion travailed, she brought forth her children.*

*The enabled body* is a call to unity by intercessory prayer, fasting and obedience in His word.

Angie Elaine V. Coote is a Kingdom woman whose faith and relationship is in the Most High who is her everything. Her faith journey is continuously her assurance that Her God is superior, powerful, loving, and compassionate. Her Abba-father sees and knows our every move.

Psalms 139: 13-17. (KJV)

*I will praise thee; for I am fearfully and wonderfully made, marvelous are thy works; and that my soul knoweth right well.*

*My substance was not hid from thee, when I was made in secret, and curiously wrought in the lowest parts of the earth.*

*Thine eyes did see my substance yet being unperfect; and in thy book all my members were written, which in continuance were fashioned, when as yet there was none of them.*

*How precious also are thy thoughts unto me, O God! How great is the sum of them!*

Elaine is an encourager to the Body of Christ with a compassionate love for humanity. She is an alumna graduate of Caribbean Christ for the Nations Bible Institute. She earns an Associates Diploma in Theology.

She is trained and certified as a Practical Nurse, Nursing Assistant, inclusive of a Patient Care Technician Course.

www.ingramcontent.com/pod-product-compliance
Lightning Source LLC
LaVergne TN
LVHW011732060526
838200LV00051B/3143